The Frazzled Mother's Guide to
INNER PEACE

THE
FRAZZLED
mother's
GUIDE TO
INNER
PEACE

PAT BAKER

Tyndale House
Publishers, Inc.
Wheaton, Illinois

Unless otherwise indicated, Scripture quotations
are from *The Living Bible*, copyright 1971 held by
assignment to Illinois Regional Bank N.A. (as
trustee). All rights reserved. Other Scripture
quotations are from *The Holy Bible*, King James
Version (KJV) or *The Amplified Bible* (AMP), Old
Testament copyright 1965, 1987 by The
Zondervan Corporation. The Amplified New
Testament copyright 1958, 1987 by The Lockman
Foundation. Used by permission.

Library of Congress Catalog
Card Number 88-51857
ISBN 0-8423-0926-8
Copyright 1989 by Pat Baker
All rights reserved
Printed in the United States of America

3   4   5   6   7   8   9   10   95   94   93   92   91   90

Pamela, Dana, and Beth,

It seems appropriate to show my respect and admiration for you as mothers by dedicating this book to you, since you are my "gifts from God."

If those gifts weren't enough, you filled my nest again with grandchildren:

Julia,
Brian,
Jim,
and Michael.

They stirred up my mother heart again, as I knew within hours after their birth that they had become my "extra gifts from God." You're doing a wonderful job with my grandchildren.

Love, Mom

Contents

Preface:
So This Is
Motherhood!

Seventy-two hours after my first baby was born, as hard as I tried, I couldn't convince myself that I would survive motherhood. For several months before my daughter was born I honestly believed my maternal instincts would surface naturally, everything I had read in Dr. Spock's book would come true, and I would be the first Perfect Mother recorded in history.

My baby cried a lot. She wasn't accepting life outside of my womb too well. *I* cried a lot. I wasn't accepting my role as a mother too well. My daughter made so many noises the little time she did sleep that I knew at any minute she'd wake up hungry. I'd run to heat her bottle, and by the time it was ready to serve, she was still asleep. Whenever she was awake I thought I should be doing something with her: feeding, rocking, walking with her, talking to her . . . never realizing that she might enjoy being left alone for a few minutes.

I got so weary of my new job, lost so much sleep, knew I'd be the first drop-out from the class of parenting, that I told my husband, through tears, that I *knew* I was losing my mind.

Obviously, I needed to get away from my new responsibilities, but the maternal bonding wouldn't let go. Common sense told me I needed no more than fifteen minutes a day away from everything that resembled motherhood. When I didn't follow through with that logic, I continued to experience more fatigue and more tears! I had no immediate proof that there would ever be a morning when my eyes wouldn't burn due to lack of sleep.

I stayed so busy that I can't remember whether I prayed much. I sure didn't have time to read my Bible. I probably couldn't have found it, anyway. But then something happened. I didn't plan it and didn't know I needed it.

One cold winter evening, I became so desperate to get away from motherhood that I handed my new role to my husband, opened the door to our large walk-in closet, went in, closed the door, sat on a small stool, and bowed my head. I was too tired to talk and even too tired to cry.

I don't know how long I sat there before I started to talk with God. I longed for him to convince me that I wasn't going to fail motherhood, that all the volunteer hours I was checking off as a new mother were important, that I was important, and that I was *not* losing my mind.

When I left my closet, God had convinced me that I was to continue my life where I'd left off only moments before. He assured me that I'd get better at being a mother and that he would help me over the rough spots.

That night, in my closet, God let me know that being a mother would be the most significant role I would ever play. The responsibilities would be so heavy I couldn't carry them alone. He impressed on me the need to take some breaks from my job so I could be alone with him, no matter what time of day, no matter where I was, even if I had only a few minutes to spare. I was to have *Closet Time* with him. During that time I would listen to his instructions and he would clue me in on the plans he had for my baby, my husband, and me. Closet Times were definitely to be part of motherhood.

CATEGORIES OF MOTHERS

I don't know how you categorize yourself as a mother, but over the years I've discovered that there are two categories of new mothers. It shouldn't take you long to learn which category fits you.

Category One: These are the mothers who enter their babies in parades and baby contests by the time the babies are eight weeks old. They've introduced their babies to swimming pools, libraries, shopping malls, movie theaters, football stadiums, and amusement parks during that same eight week interval.

These women are out jogging just a few days after delivery, are entertaining guests around playpens and breast pumps, have joined the work force outside their homes, and have more energy than they had before their babies were born.

Category Two: This category includes mothers whose babies are acquainted with the four walls of home, their back and front yards, and the street that runs directly in front of their house. They have never witnessed a parade or any other event that Category One babies have seen.

Even after their six-week check-ups, these mothers are still taking sitz baths and trying to sit gracefully when company comes. They panic when a mother and her three, lively, runny-nosed children come to see the baby while he's sleeping. This mother type has the energy level of a ninety-year-old woman in poor health.

I met all the requirements for Category Two. I admired the Category One mothers, but I didn't qualify to be one of them. The only thing these categories have in common is that both need Closet Times.

USING THIS BOOK
This book is divided into phases. If you can take *three breaks a week* with this book, your baby will be six months old when you finish it. By then you'll qualify as a professional mom whether you fit into Category One or Two!

Leave your book where you spend most of your time, so it'll be handy when you're ready for a break. I pray that the words I've written and the nudging of the Holy Spirit will help you have your own special Closet Times with God.

Pat Baker

fears, frustrations, and fatigue

Coping with Your Fears

HAS the word *fear* crossed your mind lately? Maybe this definition suits you perfectly right now: "To feel painfully uncertain."

No first-time mother ever feels certain about anything as new as being in charge of a helpless baby. Reading about babies has been good for you, but it's these first six weeks of basic training on the field of parenting that produce the reality of babies and the grit it takes to care for them.

Sometimes it's awkward to hold your baby. His head bobbles around and falls on your chest if you don't have a good hold on it. You've followed the suggested procedures in your baby books, but you can't get your baby to burp or make his hiccups stop.

When he doesn't have a bowel movement for two or three days, you're afraid he might have an intestinal obstruction. When he gets a diaper rash, you wonder if you're not changing his diaper often enough or if you aren't doing the clean-up job properly.

His crying upsets you most. "Why is he crying?" "Why does he wait until nighttime to cry the longest and loudest?" You keep thinking, "If only he could talk!"

Fears are intensified because you are uncertain about this first round with motherhood and you're afraid that you aren't "cut out" for this new role. This uncertainty diminishes as you handle your baby and as you get better acquainted with his signals and habits. What you're uncertain about now will be history in a few weeks.

Identifying Your Fears

But when I am afraid, I will put my confidence in you. Yes, I will trust the promises of God.

Psalm 56:3

FEARS are normal! Any veteran mom can assure you that she experienced the same fears that you are facing. Try to identify your fears by grouping them into categories.

Fears concerning your baby. You're afraid your baby isn't getting enough to eat or he's eating too often. There's something wrong or he wouldn't be crying so much and sleeping so little. He breathes funny sometimes. Some of his bowel movements don't look right.

Fears concerning your husband. He isn't holding the baby right. He isn't spending enough time with the baby. You're afraid he thinks you're spending too much time with the baby and not enough time with him.

Fears concerning yourself. You're holding your baby too much or not enough. You're not sure if you should let him cry more. You're afraid to let someone else take care of him. You wonder who would take care of your baby if you died!

As you identify your fears, share them with your husband, and together commit them to God. Repeat Psalm 56:3 every time you fear for your baby, your husband, or yourself.

Dealing with Impossible Days

If you want to know what God wants you to do, ask him, and he will gladly tell you, for he is always ready to give a bountiful supply of wisdom to all who ask him; he will not resent it. But when you ask him, be sure that you really expect him to tell you, for a doubtful mind will be as unsettled as a wave of the sea that is driven and tossed by the wind; and every decision you then make will be uncertain, as you turn first this way, and then that. If you don't ask with faith, don't expect the Lord to give you any solid answer. James 1:5-8

YOU have read many books about eating the right foods while pregnant in order to develop a strong baby. You read books and saw at least one movie about the birth process. In the books that you read and the pictures that you saw, the mothers looked happy and confident. Their coordinated, well-fitting clothes were spotless and wrinkle-free.

These scenes hinted that your day would include a baby who would wake up just long enough to eat. You'd talk to him awhile and try to get him to smile. You'd make sure he was dry and comfortable, and then you'd lay him in his crib and he would sleep until it was time to eat again.

While your baby slept you'd have time to pursue a hobby, relax, exercise, and occasionally prepare a quiet candlelight dinner for you and your husband. *End of dream!*

No legitimate book—fiction or nonfiction—prepares you for how you will react when the scenes just described don't happen on a regular basis. They make you wonder if you're doing something wrong or if you haven't been endowed with natural maternal skills. You don't say it out loud, but there have been days when you haven't enjoyed being a mother.

When these days happen, tell yourself that motherhood has never involved all ideal days, but neither has it included all impossible days. God shares a special plan in James 1:5-8 for both impossible and ideal days.

As difficult as "impossible" days are, they are golden opportunities to practice depending on God to give you wisdom in your new role.

Establishing Equilibrium

Your Father knows

exactly what you need

even before you ask him!

Matthew 6:8

IF you could divide yourself into three sections, you would be labeled physical, emotional, and spiritual. When one of these sections gets out of balance, it affects the other two.

You have days when you're so tired you don't think you'll ever be rested again. Because you're physically tired, your spiritual section is affected because you're too tired to pray. Then your unbalanced emotional section takes over and makes you feel guilty because you can't or don't want to pray. This makes you feel that God is unhappy with you. That's a heavy, unfair thought for a new mother. But it's real to you because that's what your mind registers when you're physically tired. Try to refocus your tired mind on the promise of Matthew 6:8.

Hang on to the truth that God is equally interested in your spiritual, emotional, and physical needs. Ask God to help you identify which section may be out of balance. Be determined to do what it takes to be a whole, balanced person again.

Accepting Your Body

The Lord God formed a man's body from the dust of the ground and breathed into it the breath of life. And man became a living person.

Genesis 2:7

He . . . gives life and breath to everything and satisfies every need there is. Acts 17:25

THE thought probably hasn't occurred to you to thank God for your body since there's still some reconstruction work that must take place before you get back to your original shape. While you're working at firming up:

- Thank God that you have a body that is capable of conceiving a miracle.
- Thank him for ears that can listen for your baby when he needs you.
- Thank him for a strong back that can carry, bounce, and rock your baby.
- Thank God for the sense of touch that lets you feel the softness of your baby's skin and the warmth of his body next to yours.
- Thank him for hands that can find a place to stack one more dirty dish and throw a load of clothes into the washer.
- Thank God for your breath and let your breath remind you of the One who chose to make you a "living souls" capable of having a personal relationship with him.

Create as much silence as possible. Listen to yourself breathe. Take long, deep breaths. Each time you exhale, name your blessings, one by one.

25

Dealing with Unsolicited Advice

Bring [your baby] up with the loving discipline the Lord himself approves, with suggestions and godly advice. Ephesians 6:4

ARE you getting lots of advice from others? Are people discouraging you from giving your baby a pacifier? Has anyone told you that you shouldn't rock your baby or walk with him when he cries? Have they told you the sure cure for colic? Some of the less wise have probably advised you to let your baby "cry it out" at night.

If you're breast-feeding your baby, someone has surely told you that bottle feeding is best. If you have your baby on the bottle, someone has loaded you with guilt because you aren't breast-feeding. At least one person has hinted that you're "spoiling" your baby, but you're not sure what "spoiling" involves. The word just sounds bad!

You're consulting at least one highly recommended baby book for more advice written by a total stranger. You refer to it when some well-meaning person puts doubts in your mind about your child-caring techniques.

Call or visit a veteran mom. Ask her to share her secrets about successful parenting. Also, ask her what kind of advice she heard as a young mother and how she responded/reacted to it! Her

answers may help you relax more
when you're getting unsolicited
advice!

Asking for God's Help

*Lord, when doubts fill
my mind, when my heart
is in turmoil, quiet me
and give me renewed hope
and cheer.* Psalm 94:19

*Don't be weary in prayer;
keep at it; watch for
God's answers and
remember to be thankful
when they come.*

Colossians 4:2

BEFORE your baby was born you heard other mothers talk about some of their bad days with their babies. Since you didn't have a baby, you couldn't grasp the full implications of what they were saying.

How do you define "bad day" now? Is this definition appropriate: "When *nothing* goes right"?

You got some hints of your first bad day when you got up one morning and for no reason started crying. You felt like a slob! Most of the baby's clothes were dirty, and as you were putting them into the washer, you discovered there was no detergent.

You left that dismal mess and headed for the kitchen. Dry cereal didn't really appeal to you, but you were hungry and didn't want to take time to fix a warm breakfast. You opened the refrigerator door to get the milk. *No milk!* The scene continued to develop into darker shades of gray, and it was still early morning. The whole day was still ahead of you.

The complications come in many different shapes and sizes and at all hours of the day or night. Your energy level is at an all-time low,

and you can't convince yourself that
what you need is some time with
God. But take the time, and while
you talk with him, pray, "God,
please help me." Admit that you
can't face your miserable day alone.
You need God's help.

It's tempting to neglect your
Closet Time since the baby's needs
seem more urgent. Talk to your
husband, and both of you come up
with a workable plan that will help
you get regular Closet Time.

Experiencing God's Love

I have loved you . . .

with an everlasting love;

with loving-kindness I

have drawn you to me.

Jeremiah 31:3

DOES the baby's unpredictable schedule have you worn out? Do you still have days when you cry about "everything"? Are you frustrated because you have so little time to have uninterrupted talks with your husband?

Remember that in the middle of all your frustrations God loves you. The love and concern you have for your new child can be a constant reminder of how great God's love and concern are for you.

During your Closet Time today, pray this prayer: "Lord, there are so many things going on in my life. My body is going through some tremendous changes. It's difficult coping with constant fatigue. I'm not in the habit of staying this close to home. I can't get meals ready on time. I miss my husband. I'm secluded from daily contact with other adults. I keep telling myself that what I'm doing is important, but I'm not sure that I believe what I'm saying.

"What I need most is your assurance that I do have the ability to be a good mother and what I'm doing *is* important. And, Lord, most of all I need to be reminded of how much you love me. Amen."

Getting Away from It All

Fear not, for I am with you. Do not be dismayed. I am your God. I will strengthen you; I will help you; I will uphold you with my victorious right hand. Isaiah 41:10

IT didn't take you long to learn that babies eat often and that their crying has a purpose, but losing sleep is taking its toll on you. You *want* to enjoy your baby, but you're so tired that you can't enter your new role with much enthusiasm.

Being tired may have caused you to resent your husband. He leaves early for work each day, follows much the same routine he followed before the baby came, and his schedule has hardly changed. You have visions of him having lunch in a quiet corner at work or at some restaurant while you sit at home, still in your robe at noon, hoping no one comes to visit. You're surrounded by dirty dishes from the night before, eating a peanut butter sandwich that has no personal appeal and holding your squirming baby with your free arm. You wish you could trade jobs with him once in a while.

You've thought about getting out of the house for awhile, but you still don't feel comfortable leaving your baby with someone else, and you don't have the energy to get everything together to take the baby with you.

It's a sad, hopeless picture new

mothers paint in their minds. If these thoughts describe you, tell God about them, then thank him for the ways he's going to help you regain a new perspective on the love you have for your baby, your husband, and yourself.

If you could make three wishes, what would they be? Discuss your wishes with your husband. Let him help you make at least one of them come true.

Letting
God Carry
Your Load

*Casting the whole of your
care—all your anxieties,
all your worries, all your
concerns, once and for
all—on Him; for He
cares for you affection-
ately,* and *cares about
you watchfully.*

1 Peter 5:6-7 AMP

*Give your burdens to the
Lord. He will carry them.*

Psalm 55:22

GOD rising early" is a
phrase used several times in the
book of Jeremiah. It doesn't make
much sense until you know the
interpretation of the phrase. Picture
this scene:

You have been up with your baby
most of the night. Outside your
house and in the nursery there are
sounds that let you know another
day is beginning. But before you get
up, God comes to stand by your
bed, and leaning over, waits for you
to place the day's concerns on his
shoulders.

How does it make you feel to
learn that God "gets up" (rises
early) *before* you do? He waits for
you to place your concerns on his
shoulders so that you will be free to
enjoy helping a new life develop in
a way that honors God.

What's your greatest concern?
Close your eyes and visualize
yourself placing that concern on
God's shoulders. This frees you to be
the mother God knows you can be.

Sharing Your Job with God

Show me the path where I should go, O Lord, point out the right road for me to walk. Lead me; teach me. Psalm 25:4-5

YOU started motherhood with the unrealistic belief that your baby would be perfect. But now you notice that your baby's eyes get crossed at times. You want his birthmark to go away. His skin is easily irritated.

You want your baby to follow "the book," which includes unheard-of sleeping standards, eating habits, and mental skill development. You want him to respond positively to sound, sight, and other people.

Suddenly you become fiercely protective—an instinct that was dormant until you became a parent. You don't want your baby to have any characteristic—physical, mental, or social—that will isolate him from the norm. But if your baby followed every rule written in baby books, spoken by doctors, forced upon you by society or by well-meaning friends, you'd know exactly what to expect, and you wouldn't have to rely upon or trust anyone else to help you raise your baby.

If you haven't done it yet, invite God to help you raise your child, who, even with imperfections, will become the person God wants him to be.

Dealing with Difficult People

May the Lord of peace himself give you his peace no matter what happens. The Lord be with you all.

2 Thessalonians 3:16

EVERY first-time mother has had at least one acquaintance like this one. She has come to visit you several times. She talks with you at the grocery store; she calls you on the phone. Her countenance reminds you of dark, rolling clouds that appear before a storm. She overflows with years of experience, and she must share it with someone. You are the chosen one! When she comes to visit, you dread to hear what new advice she feels she must give you. You're never fully prepared for this personality type, so how do you react to her? Here's one way.

As she talks, block out her advice by mentally affirming yourself as a mother. Your main affirmations are: you love your baby more than anyone else could possibly love him. Your baby is unique, and unique doesn't always agree with verbal advice. You don't want your baby to be "traditional." You are raising this baby in a way that pleases God!

This occasional person may be one who (1) never had children, (2) isn't sure of, and has never been sure of, her own role as a mother, (3) didn't enjoy her children, (4) isn't happy with life in general.

As you're thinking which category this woman fits, realize that the visit will be over soon and you'll show her to the door. As soon as the door closes, you will continue your job, believing that you are raising your child "with the loving discipline the Lord himself approves with suggestions and godly advice" (Ephesians 6:5).

After a visit like the one just described, you will need a refreshing break. Look out your window or step outside. Notice whether you can see or feel the effects of the wind. Let the wind remind you that God "rides upon the wings of the wind." Each time you feel the wind, thank God for understanding your desires and dreams as a mother.

Accepting
Your New Role

Work hard and cheerfully

at all you do, just as

though you were working

for the Lord.

Colossians 3:23

[You] have become

[a gift] to God that

he delights in.

Ephesians 1:11

NEW mothers need generous portions of compliments since they feel they aren't making many contributions to the outside world. Have you felt that you're one of the noncontributing members of society? After all, look at the evidence stacked against you. The diaper pail is full, and the shelf designated for diapers is empty. You can't remember when you last changed your bed sheets. There's a strange odor in the kitchen, but you haven't had time to locate it.

Your hair needs shampooing, but you can't find time to do it. You manage to dress each day, but you still feel unattractive, especially since the buttons on your slacks and skirts are still inches away from the buttonholes. You suspect that your husband questions what you do while he's at work. By outward appearances, you wonder if you are contributing anything to anyone or if anyone notices that you're still around.

You have these thoughts because (1) shortly after your friends received the birth announcement they dropped by to see who your baby resembled, and now their visits have stopped; (2) you have more days of being alone; (3) you feel as though all you're doing is going unnoticed and you are slowly fading out of sight. *Now what do you do?*

You continue to "work hard and cheerfully at all you do, just as though you were working for the Lord" and to believe that you "have become [a gift] to God that he delights in."

Reestablish your new identity by concentrating on what you *are* accomplishing every day. Tell yourself that even though life has taken a new slant, you're totally immersed in one of the most intriguing, busiest roles you'll ever play. You *are* still alive and well, busy and productive, challenged and successful. Who else but you could make that statement?

Gaining a Better Perspective

To enjoy your work and to accept your lot in life—that is indeed a gift from God. The person who does that will not need to look back with sorrow on his past, for God gives him joy.

Ecclesiastes 5:19-20

IS your baby an early riser? If so, good for your baby, good for you. You can enjoy the world before it gets busy and complicated. You can soak up the silence before the traffic begins or the phone starts to ring. It's prime time for uninterrupted thoughts.

What do you normally think about while you're sitting in a semi-darkened room with your baby? At times you've probably wondered how many other mothers are up, doing the same thing you're doing. You've definitely noticed that the house needs attention. Other mornings you might think about your wardrobe and try to set a tentative date when you will fit into "real" clothes again. You need to get a load of baby clothes into the washer.

Stretch your mind beyond your daily thoughts. Take a quick glance into the future. Someday you will enjoy unbroken sleep. You'll be caught up with the washing, the house will stay straightened, you will wear a size ___ again. In the future your job will have fewer demands, but along with these luxuries will come a little child old enough to slip his hand from yours

and start off to school. There will be
others to take care of many of his
needs. Do your best to concentrate
on today and the joy it holds.

It will be a busy day, so include
God in it. "Lord, when it would be
so easy to resent all I have to do,
help me understand that it's a
privilege to have this new day. Help
me remember that babies don't stay
babies, and that they do start
sleeping through the night
eventually. I don't want to dread all
that's facing me today. I want to
enjoy my baby. I'm asking you to
give me a grateful heart for all that I
have been given, even my work.
Amen."

Getting Some Rest

It is senseless for you to work so hard from early morning until late at night . . . God wants his loved ones to get their proper rest. Psalm 127:2

RECEIVING enough rest was no problem until those last two months of pregnancy. Sleeplessness should have been your clue for "things to come."

Soon after your baby's birth, he formed the habit of waking up somewhere around 2:00 A.M. daily, needing to be fed. You thought, "Why can't this baby sleep longer between feedings?"

When you answer his morning calls, you stumble into his room, turn on as few lights as possible since your eyes are burning from lack of sleep. You hold your wide-eyed, well-adjusted baby and ask yourself, "Will I ever feel rested again?"

After you're up for only a few minutes there's still a physical heaviness lingering that won't go away until you can rest again. This is when determination takes charge. You make a resolution: "Sometime today I *will* rest."

Follow through with this resolution by refusing to walk through the house and look at the work that's calling for your attention. Unless you have live-in help (What a wonderful thought!), the housework will wait until you have rested. Your work load won't look impossible since you'll see it through rested eyes.

As soon as your baby goes to sleep, lie on the floor. Inhale slowly through your nose. Continue to inhale until your lung and stomach areas are full of air. Hold five seconds. Exhale slowly for five seconds, first exhaling the air from the rib section, then the stomach section. Wait two seconds and repeat this breathing exercise ten more times. Caution: If you do this exercise with your eyes closed you may fall asleep. If you do, congratulate yourself when you wake up.

Releasing Worry

Don't worry about anything; instead, pray about everything; tell God your needs, and don't forget to thank him for his answers. If you do this, you will experience God's peace, which is far more wonderful than the human mind can understand. His peace will keep your thoughts and your hearts quiet and at rest as you trust in Christ Jesus.

Philippians 4:6-7

EVERYONE has the same kind of built-in emotions, but you have one emotion that works overtime. Worry. You worry about things you never dreamed you would ever worry about. They usually appear in full force at the end of a busy day, and they come in different degrees.

You worry when you can't find time to take out the trash, the furniture needs dusting, the refrigerator needs cleaning, and you don't have time to prepare the kinds of meals you know you're capable of preparing.

You worry about the diminishing bank balance. You can't imagine where the money is going since you have such little time to shop anymore.

You worry that so few people drop by to visit. And then you worry that someone really might visit and see your mess.

You worry about your health. "How will I care for my baby if I get sick?"

You worry about your baby's health.

You worry about worrying. "I shouldn't worry, but I can't help it."

Close your eyes. Think about your

worries. Tell God, "I'm worried about _____ ." Ask God to take control and help you dispose of the worries so they won't rob you of the enjoyment that he has meant for you to have.

Accepting God's Grace

HOW does your house look? Does it give you a queasy feeling in the pit of your stomach that says you might not get it straightened before someone comes?

Have you rated yourself a "bad mother" because the baby doesn't (1) sleep more, (2) cry less, (3) have a schedule yet, etc.?

Did you dream of being the perfect mother and now find your expectations impossible to fulfill? Do you consider yourself a boring person because your conversation consists of disposable diapers and baby food bargains and how many diapers your baby goes through in a day?

You wanted a Superbaby, but your baby has indicated that he can't be, and doesn't want to be, connected with that name?

Bring your thoughts with you to your Closet Time. Tell God how each thought is making you feel. And even if it takes longer than usual, stay in your Closet Time until you get some relief from what's bothering you. Everything else can wait.

Accepting Yourself

Thank you for making me so wonderfully complex! It is amazing to think about. Your workmanship is marvelous—and how well I know it. You were there while I was being formed in utter seclusion! You saw me before I was born and scheduled each day of my life before I began to breathe. Every day was recorded in your Book! Psalm 139:14-16

WHILE you were a student, you may have tried to make A's on your report card, but you were a B or C student. You continually tried to be on the starting team of something or be chosen for the lead in a class play. Instead, you were chosen as a sub or you made a great supporting actress. How you longed to be a number one, once in your life.

Similar desires continue into motherhood. You've discovered mothers who are organized and calm. They appear to have all the answers, and you want so much to be like them. Some mothers are poised in any group situation, able to carry on a conversation about anything. How you would like to be like them!

You see young mothers whose figures are trim; there's no lipstick smear on their chin, no catsup in the corners of their mouth, and their outfits always match. You wonder, if you walked into their homes at sunrise, would their hair be perfectly styled and their makeup on? How you would like to look like them!

Other mothers have their beds made and everything in its place by

7:00 A.M. each day. How many times
you have wished your house looked
like theirs!

You've seen these women only
briefly. You have no way of knowing
how many of these mothers you've
seen talking in groups wish they
could be better listeners . . . like
you. Other mothers wish they could
be more flexible and not feel as
though they had to keep their
houses straightened. They've come
to your house to visit, and they've
yearned to be more tolerant of a
cluttered house . . . like yours.
These potential Mrs. Americas wish
they could feel comfortable in jeans,
no makeup, and bare feet . . . like
you.

Dear mother, your days are so
busy and going by so quickly. Please
resolve to avoid wishing to be like
someone else, and believe that God
loves you just the way you are. He's
perfectly satisfied with the
personality he has given you. He
enjoys your natural beauty even
when you're avoiding all mirrors.
He takes great pleasure in his
creation of you . . . no duplicates
. . . just you.

God not only sees the masses he
created, he sees *you*, and what he
sees in you, he loves!

PHASE TWO

some new break- throughs

Establishing Priorities

So don't be anxious about tomorrow. God will take care of your tomorrow too. Live one day at a time. Matthew 6:34

THINK back to the day you were left completely alone to take care of your baby. The care giver you had depended on for several days left. She had worked around the clock so you'd have time to rest and become more confident handling your baby. She cooked the meals and did the housework. She guarded your time by taking phone messages.

Miraculously, after she left, you managed to keep the baby's clothes washed, dried, folded, and put away. You planned and cooked meals, shopped, and still had time to take care of your baby—most of the time. There were other days when nothing went right and you felt overwhelmed.

You know the budget could never manage a full-time "Nannie," but you feel there's no way one person can be expected to keep doing all you're doing. Then the thought hits you, "I don't have to do all this stuff in one day. What am I trying to prove? No one's pushing me but me." That's a healthy thought; hold on to it.

Identify your priorities by fitting your work load into three main categories: baby's needs, husband's needs, and your needs. Anything that doesn't fall into one of these categories can wait. God means it when he tells you not to look past today.

Getting Revitalized

Morning by morning he wakens me and opens my understanding to his will. The Lord God has spoken to me and I have listened. . . . Because the Lord God helps me, I will not be dismayed; therefore, I have set my face like flint to do his will, and I know that I will triumph.

Isaiah 50:4-5, 7

SOMEONE needs to tell you that it is not an act of betrayal to take regular breaks from motherhood. They're your lifesaving devices.

This is difficult to do because you honestly think you're indispensable to your baby, but you must also think that there are others capable of caring for your baby, even if it's for only a few minutes. During that time away you will be revitalized.

During your break, if you need some physical exercise, do it. If you want to visit someone, do it. If you have a desire to be alone with God, do it. Your personal needs didn't end when you became a mother, but it's easy to lose yourself in parenting and neglect those needs. Since personal neglect is a common disease among new mothers, ask God to give you wisdom to understand your needs, and then make sure you do something about them. Isaiah 50:4-5, 7 will help you get started.

What would you like to do today more than anything else? What arrangements would you have to make to do it? Ask your husband or a friend to help, and do it!

Measuring Success

[Keep on] asking God to help you understand what he wants you to do; asking him to make you wise about spiritual things; and asking that the way you live will always please the Lord and honor him, so that you will always be doing good, kind things for others, while all the time you are learning to know God better.

Colossians 1:9-10

SOME of your days start out looking so promising. You get a hint that your baby is getting on a schedule. However, when you become confident he's scheduled himself to take two long naps each day and to go to sleep early in the evening, he reverses his strategy and starts taking several short naps through the day and stays up until the ten o'clock news . . . or later. You're convinced that you'll never be sure of having a dependable schedule. When you turn in your daily worksheet, it doesn't look like you've done much, due to all of the unscheduling throughout the day.

To answer any doubts that you may have about these kinds of days, concentrate on looking past everything that didn't get done and think about the time you spent caring for your baby. Now pray, "Lord, I need you to help me understand that there's no need to get down on myself when I don't think I'm getting anything done. I keep asking you to help me understand what is important so I won't have to wonder at the end of each day if I've done what you wanted me to do. I long to be a good mother. Thank you for understanding my desires."

Make this resolution: "I will absolutely refuse to be annoyed by anyone or with anything today . . . even an interrupted schedule."

A Healthy Self

*Use every part of your
body to give glory back to
God, because he owns it.*

1 Corinthians 6:20

THE world's definition for success is "stay busy and produce." To comply with this standard, your daily list of things to do reads: "straighten house," "do the wash," "make phone call," "get groceries," but you don't write "rest," because being a "success" doesn't include time to rest. There's too much to do. With that thought, you defy the one law of nature that declares that every new mother owes it to herself and to her family to rest.

Brush up on what you learned in those boring health classes while you were a student. To have a strong body, get plenty of fresh air (but you think, *I can't go outside, I have to listen for the baby),* regular exercise (you convince yourself, *I get all the exercise I need walking with the baby around the house),* adequate food (you rationalize, *I don't have time to plan meals that require lots of time),* sufficient rest (you convince yourself, *About the time I lie down, the baby will wake up),* and relaxing recreation *(Sounds great, but everyday? I have too much to do).*

Here's instant proof how you can fulfill three of these five health requirements at the same time. It takes approximately ten minutes a day to do it.

Before your husband goes to work or after he comes home, take a brisk ten-minute walk. In that time you meet the minimum daily requirements for fresh air, exercise, and relaxing recreation. Two requirements are left. For the adequate food requirement, dust off the crock pot and stir up some nutritious recipes. Sufficient rest is the last requirement. To meet this one, take the opportunities to rest when they appear.

You Make a Difference

Then these righteous ones will reply, "Sir, when did we ever see you hungry and feed you? Or thirsty and give you anything to drink? Or a stranger, and help you? Or naked and clothe you? When did we ever see you sick or in prison, and visit you?" And I, the King, will tell them, "When you did it to these my brothers you were doing it to me!"

Matthew 25:37-40

YOU'RE a wonderful mother, but it's evident that there are no awards being given for "wonderful." You aren't even receiving minimum wage for being wonderful.

If you feel you should be making a more significant contribution to the world other than "just being a mother," you need to take an overdue Importance Inventory.

How many lives have you touched within the last twenty-four hours? Your husband's? Baby's? Neighbor's? Phone caller's? Postman's?

Pick a person and think of one way God used you to touch that person's life. While you're thinking, don't overlook a smile, a compliment, or a word of encouragement. During these weeks you're seeing the value of small acts while you're "just being a mother." By remaining faithful in these acts, others are seeing God living and loving through you. You *do* make a difference!

Anticipating God's Blessings

Give thanks [to God] for all he's going to do. . . . This is good and pleases the Lord.

1 Timothy 2:1, 3

God . . . giveth us richly all things to enjoy.

1 Timothy 6:17 KJV

As a child, your parents probably reminded you to say thank you *after* someone had done something nice for you or had given you a gift. The Bible teaches us to give thanks *before* we are given anything.

Instead of asking God for more patience, thank him for the patience he's *going* to give you.

If your day of accomplishments gets stuck on zero, thank him for the kind of day he's *going* to give you.

If your workload looks impossible, thank him for how he's *going* to help you get some of it done.

If your baby requires more attention than you want to give him, thank God for how he's *going* to help you see the fringe benefits of spending time with your baby.

If it's been awhile since you and your husband have spent time together, thank God for the way he's *going* to give you a time slot with each other.

Thank God for some of the blessings he's given you since you became a mother.

Facing New Challenges

Work hard and cheerfully at all you do, just as though you were working for the Lord.

Colossians 3:23

YOUR life used to be so simple! You were satisfied with your personal appearance and confident with your job. You welcomed challenges, set goals, and met them.

Now you're faced with different challenges. You're challenged to help your body resume its original shape. Your newly acquired, drooping flab will not go back into place on its own. It requires exercise, determination, and patience.

You're challenged to stay ahead of dirty diapers and dishes. Your most unexpected challenge is picking up evidence all over the house that indicates that your baby requires more living space than you ever dreamed he would need. Fixing meals and getting to eat what you fix are daily challenges.

These new challenges have invaded your once simple life, but these are the challenges conferred upon you as a mother. Enjoy them instead of thinking of them as more mountains of drudgery to climb! You please God as he watches you deliver top-quality performances.

Someday soon meet one of these challenges head on by declaring "Stomach, Hips, and Thighs

Restoration Days." Admit that these
parts won't firm up on their own.
You've read about exercises, but
turning the pages of the book
doesn't firm up what's sagging. Use
three minutes a day to shape up and
then add more minutes as they
become available. Exercise while
your baby is awake. Your
movements will probably keep him
entertained.

Accepting
God's Peace

He will keep in perfect

peace all those who trust

in him, whose thoughts

turn often to the Lord!

Isaiah 26:3

YOU probably stayed concerned about your weight during most of the nine months of your pregnancy. You secretly wondered whether or not your husband still loved you during your shapeless state. You wondered if those stretch marks and enlarged ankles would ever go away. You read about birth abnormalities and wondered if your baby was developing properly.

Were you afraid you might not be brave during labor and the baby might not have a safe delivery? Were you concerned that your baby would get mixed up with another mother's baby at the hospital and you'd raise her child while she raised yours?

What about those concerns now? You *are* losing your extra weight. You know you are because you no longer have to ask your husband to help you put on your shoes. When you have time to look, you notice traces of stretch marks, but they don't seem as important anymore. Your delivery *was* an experience you'll never forget, and there's no doubt that your baby has unmistakable family resemblances.

God understood all of your fears. When other fears come, include

God in them. If you make a practice
of telling God your fears, "you will
experience God's peace. . . . His
peace will keep your thoughts and
your heart quiet" (Philippians 4:7).

Do you have a fear? If the fear
materialized, what's the worst thing
that could happen because of it? Do
you honestly believe God is capable
of handling the fear? How? Talk to
God about your fear and ask him to
give you peace as you hand your
fear over to him.

Dealing with Anger

Why are you cast down, O my inner self? And why should you moan over me and be disquieted within me? Hope in God and wait expectantly for Him; for I shall yet praise Him, Who is the help of my [sad] countenance, and my God.

Psalm 43:5 AMP

HAVE you had any unexpressed anger toward your *husband* since the baby came? Maybe you've thought, "He could at least hang up his clothes, make the bed, offer to bring dinner home or prepare it occasionally, stop reading the newspaper and watching television so much, and give *me* some time off." But he doesn't seem to notice your needs.

Have you been angry with *yourself?* You had always prided yourself on your personal appearance and your efficiency. Now you have broken fingernails. Your regular clothes are too tight and your maternity clothes are too loose. Your efficiency in anything is registering below normal.

You don't have the nerve to say it outloud, but you may feel anger toward your *baby.* He demands so much time, even on his good days. He has a habit of needing your attention when you had planned to do something else. You wonder how you could feel anger toward him.

Some of your anger comes because your new maternal role stops you from doing some of the things you want to do when you want to do them. Since parenting is new to your husband, he won't know what makes you angry unless you tell him! Read that sentence again. Your husband really *can't* read your mind.

When you go into your Closet Time angry, your first healthy step is to admit you're angry. Your next healthy step is to decide why you feel anger, and third, to ask God to help you deal with it.

Your husband has faced a lot of adjustments, too, and he may be feeling some frustration and anger of his own. Now that you have begun to deal with your anger in a healthy way, discuss it with your husband and give him an opportunity to tell you what he's been feeling, too.

God's Presence

And the Lord will guide you continually, and satisfy you with all good things, and keep you healthy too; and you will be like a well-watered garden, like an ever-flowing spring.

Isaiah 58:11

TODAY may have the word *hopeless* written across it. But do the unordinary. Look past and above everything that is reminding you of work. While your sights are raised, concentrate on being with God and God being with you.

Whether your day is filled with interruptions, distractions, and hard, unappreciated work, or whether it becomes quiet, peaceful, and uncomplicated, God is with you in whatever type of day it winds up being.

Remind yourself of the basic truth "God made the world." You and your baby are an important part of it. Because God made everything, he knows what each part needs. He is in control of your needs.

Days look hopeless through the eyes of a tired mother. Maybe you're in desperate need of a rest. Negotiate with your husband so you can sleep in over the weekend. You might even consider going out for breakfast alone.

Evaluating Your Productivity

She has done what she could. Mark 14:8

SOME mornings you wake up feeling that you're going to get something accomplished. You plan to fix your husband a decent breakfast, but before you even start, the baby wakes up to eat. While you feed the baby, your husband eats a bowl of cold cereal and hurries off to work.

Another day it looks like you might get to take a shower and shampoo your hair. Such a simple goal! You get in the shower and about the time you work the shampoo into your hair, the phone rings. You hurriedly wrap a towel around your head and one around your body. You grab the phone. You say to the caller, "No! I'm not interested in registering for a trade school at this time." You hang up the phone and pray no one comes before you get your hair rinsed and dried.

Another day you get a sudden burst of energy to get some serious housework done. It looks like you might get the entire house straightened in one day, but halfway through this noble endeavor your baby gets fussy, so you settle for straightening just one room.

During the evening you evaluate

your day. You try to remember if you finished any job you started. You were so determined to make the day more productive, but you have to admit that you didn't accomplish very much.

While there's little outward evidence that you have been busy all day, you can't deny that you have a satisfied customer in your arms or crib. No matter what standards the world uses to judge productive manpower, you have used the abilities and time that God has given you to honor him through your caring. He will never ask any more of you.

In God's Word, when Mary washed Jesus' feet with an expensive perfume she was criticized by the disciples for being wasteful. The act they considered wasteful, Jesus considered a reflection of this woman's generous heart. Her heart was so full of love for her Savior that it had to find expression. Her action was explained in this simple way: "She has done what she could."

Parenting can get heavy! The heaviness sometimes causes a mother to misplace her sense of humor. Maybe it's time to check out and read a humorous book from the library. One of the best books out is *I Lost Everything in the Postnatal Depression* by Erma Bombeck.

Dealing with the Unpredictable

For I have learned to be content (satisfied to the point where I am not disturbed or disquieted) in whatever state I am. Philippians 4:11 AMP

Don't be upset. Expect God to act! For I know that I shall again have plenty of reason to praise him for all that he will do. He is my help! He is my God! Psalm 42:11

HAVE you had a day recently when you haven't had time to change your clothes after you noticed some spots of unknown origin on them? Maybe you're trying to find time for that candlelight dinner with your husband, but you finally decide to scratch that idea until the baby is old enough to pack his own bag and visit his grandparents overnight.

Your husband has become so sensitized to the time it takes you to be a mother that he doesn't even comment when you serve meals consisting of lukewarm hot dogs and stale potato chips.

You've lost count of how many times you've changed the crib sheets in one day or changed your clothes because the baby missed the burp pad. You've had more phone calls today than you've had in a week.

All your days aren't hectic, but while you're going through them you can't make yourself believe that your days will ever get any easier. During a hectic time, consider the verses for today.

It's therapeutic to talk with God on these hectic days. "God, this hasn't been my best day. Surely

there has been some good in it. I'm
not quite to the point where I can
thank you for it, but with your help
I am confident that tomorrow will
be better. Teach me to relax while
I'm changing the millionth diaper
and to be happy when my good
intentions don't materialize.
Amen."

Saying No

He will teach the ways that are right and best to those who humbly turn to him. And when we obey him, every path he guides us on is fragrant with his loving-kindness and his truth. Psalm 25:9-10

For God is at work within you, helping you want to obey him, and then helping you do what he wants. Philippians 2:13

BE on guard for what will happen in a matter of weeks. Everyone knows that you are extremely busy caring for your baby. But if you were active in several organizations before your baby was born, it won't be long until your phone will start ringing and people will be approaching you about getting back into the fast lane. They'll start the conversation with, "How's the baby doing?" "How are you feeling?" Then . . . "We've missed you." "We need you." "The club may fold up if you don't come back to help us."

Face it! These statements are green-light ego builders. You haven't had compliments like these in the line of parental duty. All the things these people are saying are true. You have been missed because of your leadership abilities, your creative ideas, your enthusiasm. You are an asset to any organization, but . . .

Now is the time to drag out the art of hesitation when you're tempted to answer yes to anyone before you're ready to take on anything other than caring for your baby. A few weeks ago you only had to consider your own and your husband's interests. Not now! Ask God to give you wisdom when faced with outside opportunities.

If there's even a hint of doubt as to whether it's time to add anything else to your schedule, delay your decision. Thank your friends for thinking of you. They'll probably admire you for saying no at this time and wish they could say that word as graciously as you did.

Joy in the Everyday Tasks

Children are a gift from
God; they are his reward.

Psalm 127:3

YOU want to succeed at being a good parent, and you want to see positive end-results of your work. As far as you know, you're mixing all the necessary ingredients into your baby's life to help him succeed. Is all this work getting monotonous, or are you still having fun? Here's a sure way to test monotony versus fun.

When you feed your baby, do you think, "When he gets through eating, I'll lay him down and pray he'll go to sleep so I can wash the dishes and make the beds and then I can . . . and then . . . and . . ."?
OR
Do you concentrate on the moment and think of how the food is satisfying your baby and helping him grow and you're the one making it happen?

When it's time to give your baby a bath, do you procrastinate doing it because it takes so much time? You have to get out so much stuff, which is just more stuff to put away.
OR
As you wash that little body and get the blanket fuzz from between his fingers, toes, and creases, do you enjoy watching him squirm and

respond to the warm water and to the baby lotion that will make him feel good all over?

When you change his millionth diaper, does it cross your mind, "I wonder when he'll stop having to be changed so often so we won't have to spend so much money on diapers"?
OR
Do you imagine how good it feels to your baby to have on a clean, soft diaper?

When you talk to your baby, do you do it because the books tell you that you're supposed to talk to him?
OR
Do you do it because you can hardly wait for him to respond to your voice and know that you're the one who will make the response happen?

These jobs have everything to do with attitude. You've been performing these jobs for several weeks. As often as you do them, it isn't a surprise that they do get monotonous.

You may need a fresh start. Consider this definition of *enjoy:* "To have a good time, to take pleasure or satisfaction in." Now that you know what it means, make a conscious effort to enjoy your baby. Warning: It could become habit forming.

Putting God First

But seek for (aim at and strive after) first of all His kingdom, and His righteousness [His way of doing and being right], and then all these things taken together will be given you besides.

Matthew 6:33 AMP

WHAT have you accomplished today? Maybe while you were feeding your baby, your husband got up and started getting ready to go to work. While you were still in your robe you fixed breakfast, and by some miracle, you had time to eat with your husband. You started the washing, stacked the dishes, made up the bed, kissed your husband good-bye, and told him to hurry home from work.

In between these activities, you may have thought, "I still haven't lost the weight I gained while I was pregnant. There's no way I can justify a new wardrobe." "Sometime today I must go to the store. I don't think I can explain leftovers for the third time." "Wouldn't it be great if I could manage to have someone come once a week or every other week to clean the house?" "What can I do differently today that will help me get more things done?"

These are worthy thoughts, but there's a fine line between those thoughts and the kind of thoughts God teaches his children. He teaches about seeking his kingdom first! This truth is understood through God's perspective; otherwise, work and desires versus "seeking his kingdom first" get out of balance.

Give God first place in your day, *then* decide how new wardrobes, groceries, weight loss, and a clean house fit in. This is absolutely the most perfect plan ever conceived for living a contented, joyful life.

Being Faithful

No good thing will he

withhold from those who

walk along his paths.

Psalm 84:11

Just tell me what to do

and I will do it, Lord. As

long as I live I'll

wholeheartedly obey.

Make me walk along the

right paths, for I know

how delightful they really

are. Turn me away from

wanting any other plan

than yours. Revive my

heart toward you.

Reassure me that your

promises are for me, for I

trust and revere you.

Psalm 119:33-35, 37-38

BE your own cheering section. Admit that you've developed a fairly workable daily routine. Your baby still needs you at inconvenient times, but that's part of the routine. You're planning meals that won't ruin if you have to stop in the middle of preparing them. You've discovered short cuts to housework, figured out the best time to go to the grocery store. Your routine considers this new little person living at your house. He's the one who has helped you create a flexible Time Management Program.

Has this thought crossed your mind, "Is what I'm doing really going to be that significant in my baby's life and my life in a few years?"

Remember what happened to Moses after he was accused of killing an Egyptian? He ran away to the land of Midian. During the next forty years Moses worked as a shepherd. He had lots of time to think and to pray as he took care of his sheep.

He probably followed the same daily routine: Get up early. Find pasture where the sheep can graze. Find water for them to drink. Make sure each sheep is safe. Without

Moses being fully aware of the significance of his job, God was preparing him for a job promotion. In God's timing, Moses was elevated from the quiet life of a shepherd to the leader of thousands of people.

Moses' claim to fame wasn't recognized by *what* he did but by *how* he did his job. He was as faithful at being a shepherd in those quiet hills of Midian as he was faithful at leading the Israelite children out of captivity.

Take this thought to bed with you at night and get up with it each morning, "I will be faithful in *whatever* I do. God will give me other jobs to perform later because that's his way of using, blessing, and honoring a person who has been faithful to him." That's a promise.

In God's Presence

The one thing I want from God, the thing I seek most of all, is the privilege of meditating in his Temple, living in his presence every day of my life, delighting in his incomparable perfections and glory. Psalm 27:4

LORD, I haven't been in touch with you much since the baby came. I haven't always known what jobs to leave off so I could have regular times with you, but I have some time now and I want to thank you for walking me and my family through these past weeks.

"Thank you for believing in a new mother like me.

"Thank you for relieving me of many of my fears.

"I've cried often. Thank you for understanding my tears and for giving them to me to wash away frustrations and impatience.

"Thank you for your presence through the long nights.

"Thank you for the reassurance that I'm not in this profession alone.

"I have felt perfectly free to admit to you that I've gotten tired of being a mother at times, that I still get aggravated with my husband for not being around when I need him. Even though my baby has captured my time, my thoughts, and my heart, I get disgusted with myself for thinking that I'll never be free from so many responsibilities. I had no idea this job would be so hard.

"I've definitely made some new breakthroughs as a mother, and

now I'm ready to tackle the days
ahead since I finally figured out that
I don't have to perform this job
alone. I love you, Lord. Amen."

Congratulations! You've made it
through another phase of motherhood. Praise God for his continued
faithfulness as you step into phase
three!

PHASE THREE

better days... and nights

Checking
Your Attitude

*I have learned the secret
of contentment in every
situation . . . for I can do
everything God asks me
to with the help of Christ
who gives me the
strength and power.*

Philippians 4:12-13

IT'S Attitude Checkup Time. Check the phrases, if the *majority* of the time you're:

_____ unhappy with what you're doing

_____ happy with what you're doing

_____ angry because you're husband isn't doing all you think he should be doing as a husband/dad

_____ grateful for the many things he is doing to help

_____ irritated because your baby isn't sleeping well

_____ thankful for the time he does sleep

_____ expecting too much out of yourself

_____ accepting yourself for what you *can* do in twenty-four hours

_____ displeased with your personal appearance

_____ pleased with the exercises you're doing that you know will help you resume your former shape

_____ aggravated with all the interruptions that come

throughout the day
_____ resourceful with your
uninterrupted time

Study your answers. Congratulate yourself on your good attitudes. Decide what attitude needs the most work.

Discovering Your Worth

Be sure to use the abilities God has given you. . . . Put these abilities to work; throw yourself into your tasks so that everyone may notice your improvement and progress.

1 Timothy 4:14-15

THINK of the qualities you like about yourself. Admit one of them out loud. You look as attractive without makeup as with it. People remember you for your smile. You're energetic. You like to see things get done right. You have a contagious laugh.

Look a little deeper. You could be described as a sensitive and compassionate person. You cry for and with others who are going through difficult times. You give generous portions of your time to people, and prefer to remain anonymous in what you do for them. You have a great sense of humor. You're a faithful wife, friend, and confidante. People feel comfortable with you. You make them feel necessary.

One step deeper. You long to please God by using all the outer and inner gifts he has attached to your wholeness. You believe that God is pleased with how he made you and that he wants you to use your special inner gifts to bring glory to him.

Doesn't it sound reasonable that you have no other option than to discover daily, and then hang on to, how much you're worth in Christ?

Think of five good things about
yourself and thank God for them.
Then share them with your
husband. You're not bragging.
You're simply affirming your worth
in Christ.

Redeeming Your Time

Live purposely and worthily and accurately . . . making the very most of the time.

Ephesians 5:15-16 AMP

HAVE you wondered how two people could leave so many closet doors, dresser drawers, and kitchen cabinet doors open? How could you and your husband drop or hang clothes in so many strange places? There's usually a potential load of laundry stacked in the corner of some room. You haven't prepared any four-course meals lately, so why are there so many dirty dishes? Do these scenes affect your good moods? If so, here are some household facts.

- It takes one minute to make a bed.
- After you decide which clothes are dirty or need only to be hung up, and depending on how many of these items are lying around, it takes less than 20 minutes to perform that job.
- It takes three minutes to shut the closet doors, dresser drawers, and kitchen cabinets.

Total transformation time: **34 minutes**

The encouraging part of this time plan is noticing how big jobs get small when they're broken down into minutes. You may think you don't have enough energy to do these jobs every day, but your body creates energy and feels better as you do the basic bending, stretching, and moving quickly to get your house straightened.

What are two jobs you've been avoiding? Do one of them during the next forty-eight hours. Concentrate on one job at a time. Don't answer the phone during those minutes. A person needing you will call back. Avoid turning on the television. You'll be tempted to stop what you're doing to watch a program/commercial that won't add one good thing to your day.

This 34-minute plan is not a formula just for the time you're a new mother. It affects your productivity for the rest of your life. Get busy . . . for 34 minutes.

Exploding the Perfect Baby Myth

O Lord, you are worthy to receive the glory and the honor and the power, for you have created all things. They were created and called into being by your act of will.

Revelation 4:11

NEW mothers play the game "Let's Compare Babies." It's a game devised to frustrate first-time mothers whose babies have detoured from what other babies their age are doing.

You've already heard a friend gloating (she wasn't gloating, but you thought she was) that her baby started sleeping through the night when he was five days old. *You* may still be losing count of how many times you get up with your baby.

Your baby will either weigh more or less or will be taller or shorter than other babies his age, but in the comparison game, mothers don't consider that heredity makes those differences.

At the doctor's office, you've walked the halls with your baby and tried to get him to stop crying. You've wanted to glare—and probably did—at the mothers holding their quiet, motionless babies.

For every newborn that sleeps through the night five days after birth, is the perfect weight, and sleeps anytime, anywhere, and on anything, there are ninety-nine other babies who have strayed from what the comparison game calls "average."

If every baby followed all the game rules, how could they develop that unique personality that God designed in them? So your baby is defying comparisons. Good for him! He's already finding his special place in God's perfect creation that defies comparisons.

Avoid playing "Let's Compare Babies" when you are with other young mothers. If possible, sell your "game" at a garage sale. You and your baby don't need it. God has given you a unique baby to love. Thank him for his special gift right now.

Living in His Presence

The one thing I want from God, the thing I seek most of all, is the privilege of meditating in his Temple, living in his presence every day of my life, delighting in his incomparable perfections and glory. There I'll be when troubles come. He will hide me. He will set me on a high rock. . . . Then I will bring him sacrifices and sing his praises with much joy. Lord, be merciful and send the help I need.

Psalm 27:4-7

CONCENTRATE on the truth that God is omnipresent. All of God is with you all the time. *All* of God, *all* the time. If you overlook this attribute, the parental mountains you climb every day look impossible. This visual aid may remind you of the omnipresent God.

Picture your mind divided into four parts. One part holds "baby needs," another part holds "your needs," the third, "husband needs," and the last, "everything else."

Your mind is completely full of people's needs and things to do. Somehow you must give God room to come in and fill a portion of your mind with himself. How do you do that?

You ask the Holy Spirit to take control of your mind, and that request makes room for God to fill your mind with what he knows you need. Remember that whatever happens, *all of God* is with you. He's with you because he wants you to experience his peace even while you're climbing parental mountains.

Think of a time in your life when you have personally experienced the powerful presence of God. Tell your husband or a friend about it.

Time Out

This is the day the Lord has made. [I] will rejoice and be glad in it.

Psalm 118:24

God wants his loved ones to get their proper rest.

Psalm 127:2

HAVE you tried to rest recently, but instead of resting, your mind decided to start working? Your eyes clenched shut and your body tensed. You were mentally listing, in living color, all you needed to be doing. You became more tense as you lay there, knowing you needed to rest but also knowing that your baby would probably wake up before you ever got to sleep. So you got up, trudged through two or three more hours of baby work before he was ready to go back to sleep. All you could think was, "I'm so tired!" And somewhere in the back of your mind you believed you would never feel rested again.

Today in your Closet Time, ask God to teach you to relax and to learn the art of taking time out for yourself.

How does this sound? For the next several days, as soon as your baby falls asleep *for the first time that day,* whether or not you've done anything else, allow yourself fifteen minutes to rest. Lie down and close your eyes, or sit in a chair and resurrect a hobby or read.

If your baby wakes up after the allotted fifteen minutes, you've at least given your body a recess. If your baby is still asleep after that time, continue this delicious break until he wakes. Don't give in to one minute of guilt for resting. If guilt creeps in, replace it with the thought that what you're doing gives you the physical stamina you need to make the most of the rest of the day.

101

Resting in God

[The Lord] makes me lie down in (fresh, tender) green pastures; He leads me beside the still and restful waters. He refreshes and restores my life—my self.

Psalm 23:2-3 AMP

EVEN though you expect too much from yourself, God never does. With your high expectancy, you have a persistent urge to run through the day to get everything done. As you're running, you don't have time to ask God what you're to do or not to do. Somewhere down the line you must slow down and learn what God wants you to do.

Slow me down, Lord!
Ease the pounding of my heart by
 the quieting of my mind.
Steady my hurried pace,
with a vision of the eternal reach of
 time.
Give me, amidst the confusion of
 my day,
The calmness of the everlasting
 hills.
Break the tension of my nerves
with the soothing music of the
 singing streams
That live in my memory.
Help me to know the magical
 restoring power of sleep.
Teach me the art of taking minute
 vacations of slowing down.
To look at a flower;
To chat with an old friend or make a
 new one;
To pat a stray dog; to watch a spider
 build a web;

To smile at a child; or to read from a
good book.
Remind me each day
That the race is not always to the
swift;
that there is more to life than
increasing its speed.
Let me look upward into the
towering oak
And know that it grew great and
strong
Because it grew slowly and well.

Orlin L. Crain
The Treasure Chest

Decide to take some "minute vacations" today. At the end of the day, reflect on what these minute vacations did for your overall outlook on the day, and thank God for "restoring your life" during those minutes!

Preserving Your Sense of Humor

To everything there is a season, and a time for every matter or purpose under heaven . . . a time to weep, and a time to laugh.

Ecclesiastes 3:1, 4 AMP

A glad heart makes a cheerful countenance, but by sorrow of heart the spirit is broken.

Proverbs 15:13 AMP

This is a good time to rate your sense of humor. Check the following situations that aggravate you:

_____ Phone rings and wakes baby.

_____ Phone rings while you're showering.

_____ There are two pieces of bread left . . . two sandwiches to make.

_____ Electricity goes off while blow-drying your hair.

_____ You discover you're wearing your blouse wrong side out.

_____ Someone tells you your earrings don't match.

_____ You have a run in your last pair of hose.

_____ No one has bothered to tell you that your slip is hanging three inches below your skirt.

_____ You run out of gas on the way to the store.

_____ You forget your doctor's appointment.

Hidden in most of these situations are some funny stories. You may need to dig deeper to find some of the humor but the potential for discovering it is there. Laughing at yourself doesn't always come naturally, but it *must* come eventually. Have you noticed that when you tell someone about an impossible situation, you laugh or at least smile while you tell it? That's a clue that God gave you a sense of humor and the gift of laughter that could easily get lost in a sink full of dirty dishes or in a room knee-deep with baby stuff.

Train your mind to receive messages of laughter. Practice laughing at yourself at least once a day. Laughter cleans the soul of heaviness that creeps into parenting.

Tell your husband or a friend about a ridiculous situation you've experienced lately and see if both of you can laugh about it.

Comparing Babies

Does the pot argue with its maker? Does the clay dispute with him who forms it, saying, "Stop, you're doing it wrong!" or the pot exclaim, "How clumsy can you be!"? Jehovah, the Holy One of Israel, Israel's Creator, says: "What right have you to question what I do? Who are you to command me concerning the work of my hands? I have made the earth and created man upon it."

Isaiah 45:9, 12

BY now your baby may have clearly demonstrated an instant dislike for baby food. The evidence is found on your clothing and in the slightly used jars of baby food that are molding in the refrigerator. This doesn't bother you until you hear about a baby the same age eating any food that's put in his mouth, and his mother doesn't have to squeak toys in his face to get him to open his mouth.

What do you feel when a mother tells you that it looks like her baby is about to cut a tooth and your baby's gums show no signs of teething? There will be other stages along the way to induce comparisons: sitting up, crawling, standing, walking, talking.

Comparing babies has the potential of producing children with inferiority complexes. Make this promise strong enough to last through the growing up years of your baby. Print it on paper and frame it. "I solemnly promise to allow my baby to progress at his own unique rate of growth in every area of his life, from this day forward."

Closet Times remind you to keep your eyes on Jesus, not on what

other babies and parents do. With
your eyes on Jesus, they will reflect
Jesus. In return, you will care for
your baby, accept his development
at his pace, and be responsible for
molding this little life to reflect
Jesus, not someone else's child.

Talking to God

This is too glorious, too wonderful to believe! I can never be lost to your Spirit! I can never get away from my God! . . . If I try to hide in the darkness, the night becomes light around me. For even darkness cannot hide from God; to you the night shines as bright as day. Darkness and light are both alike to you.

Psalm 139:6-12

I will pray morning, noon, and night, pleading aloud with God; and he will hear and answer. Psalm 55:17

AN important lesson you've learned since your baby was born is that when you need to pray, you don't have to close your eyes, bow your head, sit down, go to a certain room, or even kneel. Your conversations with God can occur anytime and anywhere between sunrise and sunset.

It has either been a new discovery or a rediscovery that you "can never get away from your God!" You talk with him while you're deciding which room needs the most attention, discarding moldy leftovers from the refrigerator, deciding if you have enough clean dishes to make it through one more meal, or justifying time away from being a mother.

You pray while you're in the middle of demands that absolutely won't wait. When your baby is uncomfortable with a dirty diaper, you change it, and you pray during the change. If your baby is hungry, you feed him and pray. When he cries, you hold him and pray.

You're getting comfortable talking with God, no matter what you're doing. That's the privilege he gives new mothers.

Caring for Your Husband

Don't just think about your own affairs, but be interested in others, too, and in what they are doing. Your attitude should be the kind that was shown us by Jesus Christ, who, though he was God, did not demand and cling to his rights as God. Philippians 2:4-6

SOME days you feel that anything your husband does or says is wrong. "He's not doing his share of taking care of our baby." "He's totally unaware of *my* needs. *I* need some time off, too." "At least he can get away from parenting while he's at his job. He could relieve *me* awhile, after he gets home from work."

With an inborn selfish nature hanging around, it's easier to want your needs met before you consider someone else's needs. Ignore your selfish nature for a few minutes. Think about some of the things your husband *has* done. He was never invited to the baby showers, but he was there to load up and carry in the gifts after the shower. Together you planned how to fix the nursery. He shared your days of anticipation as both of you waited to get that first look at your baby. You can only imagine how your husband felt as he coached you during the delivery.

Do you think his feelings ran as deeply as yours the first time he held that new little person in his arms? Sure, he didn't go through the physical pain you did, but he did try to empathize with you and encourage you. When the pain was over, you rejoiced together.

Unless your husband is an unusually sound sleeper, he lost sleep, too, during those first few nights after the baby came home from the hospital. He may seem unaware of your needs because everything is new to him and he doesn't know how to react to these sudden changes. He honestly doesn't know what you need. It's a sobering fact that many of his needs haven't been met either.

You will always need each other, especially now that both of you are experiencing the newness of caring for a baby whose signals aren't always clear.

Think about the attitude you have toward your husband at this time. Next, remember some of the special times you've had together. Think of the characteristics that attracted you to your husband. When you hear him come home from work, surprise him with a kiss at the door even if you're holding a crying baby.

What three expectations do you have of your husband? Are they realistic expectations? Unrealistic? Talk with your husband about expectations you have of each other. If both of you agree that some of them are unrealistic, decide what can be done about them. Then pray together about some goals you'd like to accomplish. Give each other some generous, well-deserved compliments!

Knowing God

*Do you want more and
more of God's kindness
and peace? Then learn to
know him better and
better. For as you know
him better, he will give
you, through his great
power, everything you
need for living a truly
good life; he even shares
his own glory and
goodness with us.*

2 Peter 1:2-3

QUESTION: "Do you
want more and more
of God's kindness and peace?"
Answer: "Then learn to know him
better and better." Reason: "For as
you know him better, he will give
you, through his great power,
everything you need for living a
truly good life" (2 Peter 1:2-3).

What do you need? More time? A
friend who understands how you're
feeling as a mother? A recess from
motherhood? Patience with
yourself? Peace? You've read that
you can have peace and everything
you need. The way you get both is
to get to know God better.

The way you get to know anyone
better is to spend time with them.
The same is true with getting
acquainted with God. You spend
time with him.

In the limited time you have with
God, you receive answers to your
greatest needs, and when the needs
are met, you have peace . . . even
on the most difficult days! Isn't it
great that God already knows your
needs and promises to provide
everything you need!

List your immediate needs. Hand
God your list, one by one. Expect
him to help you with each one.

Teaching Self-Esteem

You must learn to know God better and discover what he wants you to do. Next, learn to put aside your own desires so that you will become patient and godly, gladly letting God have his way with you. This will make possible the next step, which is for you to enjoy other people and to like them, and finally you will grow to love them deeply. The more you go on in this way, the more you will grow spiritually and become fruitful and useful to our Lord Jesus Christ. 2 Peter 1:6-8

WHEN your baby discovers his hands for the first time, he'll be intrigued by them. When he finds his toes, if he hasn't already, he'll ignore his crib mobile and entertain himself by playing with his toes. His eyes have already noticed and enjoyed bright lights and objects that he's never seen before. He hears his voice making coo and goo noises, and he sees your happy expressions with each sound.

You have the privilege of seeing your baby enjoy himself. How often this important lesson of self-enjoyment is overlooked, but it's one that influences how your baby will feel about himself later because his parents, in their awareness of this part of his development, helped him discover and develop the art of enjoying himself. Along with that gift follows the enjoyment of others.

Talk to your husband or a friend about ways babies can be taught healthy self-esteem. Pray together about staying aware of hidden lessons parents can teach their babies.

God's View of You

Be delighted with the Lord. Then he will give you all your heart's desires. Commit everything you do to the Lord. Trust him to help you do it and he will.

Psalm 37:4-5

WHILE you measure the success of each day by what you can actually see, God looks past your cluttered house and your slumped shoulders. He ignores your grease-spattered kitchen counters, baskets of unfolded clothes, and missing buttons and keys. He doesn't hold it against you for the way you deal with your impatience with people and things, including impatience with yourself or the way you react in the middle of the confusion that babies are accustomed to creating. Even with all this going on, God doesn't judge you by outward appearances but by the desires of your heart.

Pick an unfinished job that has been bothering you and attack it. You may need to call on your husband or a friend to help you get it done. Take advantage of their free services.

God Is
with You

*I lie awake at night
thinking of you—of how
much you have helped
me—and how I rejoice
through the night beneath
the protecting shadow of
your wings. I will rejoice
in God.* Psalm 63:6, 11

*How precious it is, Lord,
to realize that you are
thinking about me
constantly! I can't even
count how many times a
day your thoughts turn
towards me. And when I
waken in the morning,
you are still thinking of
me.* Psalm 139:17-18

EVERY day you're getting
to know God better as you meet
with him, not only in those few
minutes of Closet Times but during
all those other minutes of the day.
You've developed that sense of
awareness that God is with you as
you put clothes into your washing
machine and as you bend to get a
load of clean clothes from the dryer.
He sits with you as you fold the
clothes.

God continues to stay with you as
you try to prepare a decent meal
with a fussy baby straddled on your
hip. He's with you in your bedroom
at night as you lie in bed, and he
hears your husband tell you that
he's proud of you. He's with you
when you cry because he knows
your tears will wash away anxieties.

If it hasn't sunk into your head
and heart by now, give it the
soaking time it needs to know that
as soon as your day starts, *God is
with you.* It was never in his plan for
you to go through this special part
of your journey alone.

Making Choices

When the Holy Spirit controls our lives he will produce this kind of fruit in us: love, joy, peace, patience, kindness, goodness, faithfulness, gentleness, and self-control.

Galatians 5:22-23

PICTURE your mind divided into rooms. Some of the rooms contain worries, doubts, complaints, and criticisms. God knew you'd have these kinds of thoughts, so in his plan he gave you some choices.

You can choose to express jealousy or kindness when you hear of other babies, the same age as yours, who are a few steps ahead of yours in development. You can complain or remain calm when your workload looks impossible. You can choose to be angry or patient with people standing in line, waiting to give you free, unwanted advice. You can either complain or find satisfaction in changing diapers. You have the option of griping or rejoicing as you prepare meals for a husband who is short on compliments.

In the fifth chapter of Galatians, the writer says that there are two forces within you that will constantly fight each other to win control over you. When you follow your own desires your life will produce:

Jealousy—So what if her baby is six months ahead of schedule in *everything!*

Anger—If *you* would stay home

once in awhile, maybe *I* could get
something done for a change!

Complaints—Why do *I* always
have to . . . ?

Criticism—She probably lets her
baby cry just so she can put on her
makeup and get her nails
manicured!

Envy—Sure, being a mother is
easy for her. She has someone come
in once a week to clean her house.

On the other hand, your mind
registers the positive choices as you
consciously desire to produce the
fruits of the Spirit that God
promised you when the Holy Spirit
rules your life. This same Spirit
helps you make right choices.

Which list best describes your
"fruit production"? Concentrate on
the words of the Spirit: love, joy,
peace, patience, kindness,
goodness, faithfulness, gentleness,
and self-control. *Beautiful words!*

If some of the "fruits of the flesh"
describe you, ask God to replace
them with the fruits of the Spirit. If
your husband or a friend notices the
replacements, quietly pray, "Thank
you, Lord."

The Gift of Peace

Praise him from sunrise to sunset! For he is high above the nations, his glory is far greater than the heavens.

Psalm 113:3-4

Who can ever list the glorious miracles of God? Who can ever praise him half enough?

Psalm 106:2

WHAT'S one of the best days you've had since you became a mother? Even though you didn't get a full night's sleep; your husband was late for work because he couldn't find two socks that matched; the postman delivered most of your insurance bills; the express lane at the grocery store was closed; your washer stopped in mid-cycle; friends dropped by unannounced; it was a cloudy, dreary day . . . but you still enjoyed the day. No one could say or do anything to change your upbeat attitude. It was great to be alive!

You were grateful for the sleep you did get. You were happy that your husband had a job and socks to wear. You squeaked by with just enough money in your checking account to pay the insurance premiums on time. Waiting in line at the grocery store was good for you; it produced patience. You knew the washer could be fixed, your friends brought unexpected blessings, and you knew the sun would shine another day.

You experienced God's gift of peace that surpasses all understanding and it canceled out your fears, discouragements, and conflicts.

God's peace can never be fully explained, but it can be experienced. You know it's true because his peace invaded your life and it was good. If you haven't had a day like this for awhile, you will.

Getting Away from Motherhood

[Jesus] often withdrew to the wilderness for prayer.
Luke 5:16

The next morning [Jesus] was up long before daybreak and went out alone into the wilderness to pray. Mark 1:35

IT wasn't until you held your newborn baby in your arms, came home from the hospital, walked into the newly decorated nursery, and tried to lay your baby in his bed without waking him that you honestly felt you would never experience complete aloneness again.

Until your baby came, you could "get away from it all" with little effort. But by now you have used every strategy you can devise to have a break from motherhood. When you haven't had these breaks, life, in general, doesn't look good from any angle.

Don't apologize or feed your guilt for admitting your need to be alone. If you find yourself brushing aside the importance of aloneness, remember that Jesus gave several examples for you to follow when you need a break. Pick up on his examples and include them in your life.

Closet Times are "wilderness" times. It's the invitation you give God to hand you some special, needed blessings.

Make the necessary arrangements to go to a restaurant for a break. When you arrive at the restaurant,

order something to drink. Promise
yourself that you'll drink slowly,
something you wouldn't do if you
were at home. Look around. Study
people's mannerisms, their dress,
their expressions. Listen to the
sound of their voices. Imagine their
life-styles, jobs, interests. Soon
you'll be finished with your drink,
relaxed and satisfied with yourself,
and you'll be ready to go back
home. Those who have been
watching you will secretly applaud a
woman who obviously needed a
well-deserved break and had the
common sense to take one!

Depending on Him

*You can never please God
without faith, without
depending on him.*

Hebrews 11:6

*For when I am weak,
then I am strong—the
less I have, the more I
depend on him.*

2 Corinthians 12:10

LORD, Phase Three has
been a busy one. It's hard to believe
that my baby is growing so quickly.
I need to talk with you about
something before I get any deeper
into this job.

"I've had a few minutes recently
to think about the way you created
people, especially about the way
you started all of us out as helpless
babies, totally dependent upon
others to take care of us. We had
everything to learn, and we
depended on our parents to
teach us.

"In my Closet Times I've made a
significant spiritual breakthrough
that I want to stick with me. *To
please you, I must depend on you.*

"Be patient with me, because I
have a knack for thinking I know
what's best for everyone and
everything. I want to honor you by
admitting my dependency on you. It
makes sense that by depending on
you I will be a more confident
person.

"As I understand this dependency
on you, I accept your promise that
you will be my strength. Thank you
for that promise. Amen."

Do you have a specific need
before you enter the next phase of

motherhood? Get specific with God
and write your need on this page.
At the end of the next phase, check
back to see how God met your
need.

four months and counting

Feeling Important

So, my dear brothers, since future victory is sure, be strong and steady, always abounding in the Lord's work, for you know that nothing you do for the Lord is ever wasted.

1 Corinthians 15:58

By now, you're more than ready for someone to stop you in the store or call you on the phone and congratulate you for the good job you're doing as a mother. But most people have the annoying habit of remaining silent about the importance of your job. Television and newspapers play up the bad things that happen within families, and many of the good things are left unexposed, leaving the audience to believe that not much good happens within the family these days. With that kind of exposure, it isn't surprising that you question your importance.

You shouldn't have to paint a pro-parent banner and carry it around in shopping malls and on the streets to prove your importance, but you must regularly remind yourself that what you're doing now will make a positive impact on the world, whether or not you ever get a pat on the back or make the headlines for making it happen.

What would be your response if your husband came home today, walked into the bathroom, fixed you a warm bath, turned on some soft music, darkened the room, lit a candle, and said, "Stay as long as

you like"? Sound like heaven? Make
you feel important? Share the idea
with your husband.

Wondering What Other People Think

He will keep in perfect peace all those who trust in him, whose thoughts turn often to the Lord!

Isaiah 26:3

The Lord shall be thy confidence.

Proverbs 3:26 KJV

IS your baby using a pacifier and loving it? Does the pacifier make both of you more relaxed? The only thing that breaks the tranquility of your answer is the thought, "I wonder what people think when they see my baby sucking a pacifier?"

Your baby has developed a diaper rash. You haven't wanted anyone else to change his diaper and see the rash because you don't know what they'll think.

It's late afternoon. Your house is in the same condition it was in when you got up this morning. It shows signs that you didn't get around to any housework. "What will my husband think when he comes home?"

You had gone to the store with your baby. While you were hurriedly throwing groceries into the cart, your baby started crying. Your main concern? "What will these people think?"

Trying to comfort yourself by saying, "Who cares what other people think?" doesn't give relief because, even as you're saying it, you're extremely concerned about what they think.

Dear mother, parents who have

children the same age as yours, as well as parents of grown children know how important pacifiers are to some babies. They know it's inevitable that babies have a diaper rash sometime in their lifetime. It's one of those expected baby dilemmas. Your husband understands why the house looks the way it does. Every parent in the grocery store sweats it out with you until you get your baby to stop crying, or at least until you get out of the store.

You've made yourself miserable wondering what other people were thinking. It may or may not be news to you, but did you know that you don't have the ability to know what other people are thinking? You only think you know. With the odds being so great that you're probably wrong about the way people think, concentrate more on what God thinks about your predicaments.

Don't be too hard on yourself. It's time to give yourself a break. Several methods have been developed for encouraging rest and even sleep. Try one of them today. Close your eyes. Start with the number fifty and count backwards slowly to the number one. Or start with the number one hundred and count slowly backwards by fives. Warm milk is a relaxant. Calcium tablets three times a day (1000 mg. each) can also help with relaxation problems.

Paying Attention to Your Marriage

If I had the gift of being able to speak in other languages without learning them, and could speak in every language there is in all of heaven and earth, but didn't love others [didn't let my husband know that I still love him], I would only be making noise. [The kind of love I must have for my husband] is very patient and kind. . . . It is not irritable or touchy. . . . If you love someone . . . you will always believe in him.

1 Corinthians 13:1, 4, 7

CONSIDER this statement from Virginia Satir's book, *Peoplemaking:* "The couple has a baby, and obviously there are three where there was once two. All too often at this point the parenting becomes so weighty and demanding that the couple-life dies" (p. 203).

Your life is absorbed with your baby. You "dream" baby, "think" baby, "talk" baby, and "read" baby. Your baby has literally come between you and your husband . . . at the table, in the car, and sometimes in your bed.

You keep predicting that surely the baby will get the idea that nighttime is designed for sleep, but by the time he does go to sleep, you and your husband can hardly wait to go to bed and immediately lose consciousness with no thought for a romantic interlude.

Both of you are busy with the baby, making sure he gets the best start in life. But somewhere between the hours of sunrise and sunset, you must create time to continue your relationship with each other. Parenting does become "weighty and demanding," and much too subtly your "couple-life" starts to die, often so gradually that you and your husband may not be aware that it's dying. Sobering thought? You bet it is. Worth working on? You better believe it. When? Now!

Today as you work with your baby, "dream" husband, "talk" husband, "think" husband, and when he comes home, "love" husband in a special, unexpected way. Let him know that you believe in him. Pray for your husband now.

Wants Versus Needs

So my counsel is: Don't worry about things—food, drink, and clothes. For you already have life and a body—and they are far more important than what to eat and wear. . . . Your heavenly Father already knows perfectly well that you need them, and he will give them to you if you give him first place in your life and live as he wants you to.

Matthew 6:25, 32-33

WHAT would it take to make you happy? One room with matching furniture? A closet filled with new brand name clothing? A larger house? A new car? Steak more often and ground beef less? If you answered yes to more than half of these questions, you have qualified for Ms. Average American.

Where do these desires originate? Figuratively speaking, in society's back room. The members of this self-appointed committee push their theory that things make people happy. To complete their theory they mumble ". . . for awhile."

Your baby is not on the same level with things. This possession is not "for awhile." Your baby has been stamped with the words *Eternal Value.* He's here to give you daily reminders that *things* aren't eternal; *people* are.

So what if your furniture doesn't match, isn't even comfortable. So what if you're wearing clothing purchased at a discount store or a garage sale. Sure, your house seems smaller since you added all the baby stuff, you're hoping your car keeps running until the expense of having a baby diminishes, and you'll probably never stop asking other

mothers for more exciting ground
beef recipes.

Here are the facts that blow away
society's theory. You *need* food,
clothing, and shelter. For the next
few years these particular things
may not be luxurious, but you will
have what you *need*. Even though
the Society Committee keeps
pounding away at you, telling you
that you deserve to have the things
you want now, this doesn't mean
you won't have them eventually.
They may only be delayed for
awhile. But even if you never have
them, you *have* been promised
everything you really need.

List five of your *needs* and five of
your *wants:*

NEEDS	WANTS
1.	1.
2.	2.
3.	3.
4.	4.
5.	5.

Study your lists. Should some of the
needs go into the *wants* column?
Even if you cringe when you do it,
mark out those *needs* that should be
with the *wants*. Complete this
sentence. "Happiness is . . ."

Now read Matthew 6:25, 32-33
again.

Enduring

Don't be impatient. Wait for the Lord, and he will come and save you! Be brave, stouthearted, and courageous. Yes, wait and he will help you.

Psalm 27:14

I will try to walk a blameless path, but how I need your help, especially in my own home, where I long to act as I should.

Psalm 101:2

HAVE you prayed for patience lately? When you do so, you're praying to *endure*—to last until your baby is old enough to start school so you'll have some deserved time for yourself, or for now, to last until your husband gets home so he can take over for awhile.

You're asking to endure annoyances. Do you have any of these around your house in the form of a baby, a husband, a phone or doorbell ringing during baby's nap, housework?

You're asking to be calm without complaining. It's being calm about the jobs that aren't getting done the way you think they should be done and *when* you want them done. It's being calm when your husband has a meeting and can't spend the evening with you and the baby.

Are you enduring? Will you last? How can you remain calm and maintain a sweet spirit when you live in a house full of half-done jobs, burned meals, unmade beds, untouched dust cloths and vacuum cleaners?

What tries your patience most? What can you do about it? If something can be done, ask your husband or a friend to help you.

Experiencing Peace

I will lift up mine eyes
unto the hills, from
whence cometh my help.
My help cometh from the
Lord, which made heaven
and earth.

Psalm 121:1-2 KJV

PICTURE this scene. It's winter. You have driven to the mountains for a quiet weekend. Your reservation is confirmed at the desk and you check into your room. After you change clothes, you begin walking around outside, observing the bare black branches of the trees silhouetted against the sky. The lake is almost frozen over, and you wonder how it looks in springtime. You check out the facilities in the lodge and notice a large empty room. You go inside. Two walls of the room are enclosed with glass. Outside it's snowing. There's a large bird feeder by the window and several red birds have discovered it. The room is perfectly still except for the crackling of the burning logs in the fireplace. You are alone. You are at peace, because in your needed, deserved silence you have had a special meeting with God through his creation.

Create a quiet scene from your own life that helps you remember a time of total serenity and peace. Getting quiet could be the most revitalizing exercise you do for yourself today.

In the busyness of each day,

remember that there is a right time for everything, even "a time to be quiet" (Ecclesiastes 3:7).

Hiding God's Word in Your Heart

Forever, O Lord, your Word stands firm in heaven. Your faithfulness extends to every generation, like the earth you created; it endures by your decree, for everything serves your plans. . . . Nothing is perfect except your words. Oh, how I love them. I think about them all day long.

Psalm 119:89-91, 96-97

YOUR mind continues to be saturated with your mother role. You refer to baby books that inform you about the phases of your baby's development. You watch special television programs geared toward family. You listen to tapes about family.

This knowledge makes you more secure in your job. It's good to have this fingertip information, but sometimes your needs go deeper and can't be touched by man-made knowledge. So what's a mom to do?

Maybe it's been awhile since you read your Bible. Guilt may have been your motive when you finally found some time to read it. But it was difficult to keep your mind on what you were reading because of so many distractions. Besides, you had trouble staying awake.

God commands his children to hide his Word in their hearts because he knows that when his Word is in your heart, there's no room left for negative, defeating thoughts that creep into first-time mothers' minds. God doesn't say, "Maybe you should . . ." or "It might be a good idea if you would . . ." or "After your baby is in school why don't you think about . . ."

God knows you're busy, but it pleases him when you love and depend on his Word so much that you create time to memorize small portions of it. Nothing is impossible, even memorizing Scripture, when it's a command from God.

Perhaps the idea of anyone even suggesting that you memorize Scripture makes your stomach feel funny. It's one more thing to do, but the dividends pay well. Many of the most powerful verses in God's Word are short verses. Look at the "Scripture to Memorize" section at the back of this book. Choose a verse to memorize and repeat it on days you don't have time for Closet Time. Once you get that verse hidden in your heart, choose another one and memorize it.

It may help you memorize these Scripture verses by writing them on small pieces of paper and taping them above the kitchen sink or on the mirror. Then you can repeat them as you do the dishes or put on your make-up. Or record the verses on a tape recorder and listen to them as you're feeding or bathing your baby or as you're falling asleep.

The Cost of a Baby

Your attitude should be the kind that was shown us by Jesus Christ, who, though he was God, did not demand and cling to his rights as God, but laid aside his mighty power and glory, taking the disguise of a slave and becoming like men. And he humbled himself even further, going so far as actually to die a criminal's death on a cross. Philippians 2:5-8

ARE you still making monthly installments to get your baby "paid in full"? It didn't take long to learn that baby expenses don't end after the hospital bill is paid. The costs of having a baby are phenomenal! But other costs are just as high.

Even though your baby is older, it's been awhile since you and your husband have had more than an hour of uninterrupted time together. Your baby is costing you time with your husband.

You've given up some of your social clubs, civic organizations, and church responsibilities since your baby was born. Motherhood is costing you socially.

You can't remember when you had two hours to call your own. Motherhood is costing "alone" times.

God told the prophet Gad to tell King David that he was to go buy a threshing floor from a Jebusite man so he could build an altar to worship God. When the man heard that King David wanted to buy his threshing floor, he told David he wanted to give it to him. David replied, "No, I will not have it as a gift. I will buy it, for I don't want to

offer to the Lord my God burnt
offerings that have cost me nothing"
(2 Samuel 24:24).

Jesus didn't take any shortcuts for
you to become his child. He went all
the way . . . paid the full price.
What a sobering thought when you
think that parenting is too
demanding . . . too costly.

Have you and your husband
offered up your baby to God? If you
haven't, make plans to do it. Then,
trust God to give you and your
husband wisdom to follow the plans
he has for you as parents, no matter
what it costs. Believe that God will
do more with your baby's life than
you ever dreamed would be possible
now that you've given him back to
God.

Enjoying Yourself

*Once you were [past
tense] less than nothing;
now you are [present
tense] God's own. Once
you knew very little of
God's kindness; now your
very lives have been
changed by it.*

1 Peter 2:10

YOU'VE had your share of experiences in life that have wounded your self-esteem. You weren't very old when you found out that kids pointed out those things you were most self-conscious about and that hurt!

As a teen you weren't only self-conscious and critical of your physical appearance, but socially it was obvious that you weren't always chosen, voted for, or singled out to be what you secretly desired—a class officer, first chair in band, or a starter in sports. Even more painful was wanting to be a part of a particular group and not getting voted "in."

Then came relationships with boys. The boys you liked didn't like you, and the ones you didn't like were always hanging around.

Maybe you're one of those people who has a problem estimating your value because you are overly sensitive to the way people react toward you or to what they say to you. If you are, it's time for a change! Enjoy yourself. You're a great person to be around. When you enjoy yourself and other people, you transmit that quality of enjoyment to your baby. It's a gift you give your baby. "Be honest in your estimate of yourself" (Romans 12:3).

Memorize this verse and meditate on it whenever you are tempted to think less of yourself than God does.

A Dream Come True

Teach us to number our days and recognize how few they are; help us to spend them as we should.

Psalm 90:12

IN your wildest imagination have you dreamed for a day when you would have time to do what needed to be done as well as to have time for what you wanted to do? Pretend your dreams come true.

Early one morning, your husband stocks the diaper bag with a one day supply of diapers, milk, and baby food. He takes the baby to another destination.

As soon as they leave, you spend a few minutes trying to decide what to do first. Should you enjoy sipping a cup of coffee and reading a magazine article uninterrupted, or should you get busy with those things you've been saying you wished you had time to do?

You straighten the house. It takes only half the time because you don't have any interruptions. You clean the shower and basin. You can't remember the last time they were cleaned. As the morning progresses, you get the washing and drying done, the dishes washed, and the kitchen cleaned.

You glance at the clock and it isn't even noon. You eat an early lunch, rest for awhile, shower, and shampoo your hair.

You've learned to make better use

of your time since the baby came. Then you think of other compliments to give yourself. You spend less time at the grocery store, cook more quickly, eat ravenously, take shortcuts in clean-ups, make phone calls brief, and omit hundreds of menial jobs. None of these compliments are dreams. You are a remarkable woman. In a few short weeks you've mastered a time management course very few people have conquered.

Dream ends: Your husband walks in the house with the baby. How you missed them. Strange, but nothing you did in your dream seems important now that they're back home.

Imagine that your husband really does get the idea of offering you a whole day all to yourself whenever you want, to do whatever you want. Write down your plans for that day and share them with your husband. Is there a way that the two of you can make this day a reality?

Hug your husband for having this wonderful idea!

Sharing God's Love with Your Baby

Oh, what a wonderful God [I] have! How great are his wisdom and knowledge and riches! How impossible it is for [me] to understand his decisions and methods! For everything comes from God alone. Everything lives by his power, and everything is for his glory. To him be glory evermore.

Romans 11:33, 36

YOU'VE second-guessed yourself many times through the years, but one thing you know for sure, you love God with all your heart and you know he loves you. With a love like that you need to tell someone else about it. Your first thought? "Oh, no! Something else to do!" But you can do it! You don't have to organize an elaborate visitation program. You don't even have to leave your house. You can tell your baby about your love for God and his love for you by letting your baby hear you pray.

What an extraordinary way to spend time with your baby. Let him hear your expressions of love for God because of who he is and what he does. Let your baby hear you tell God about your desires and concerns, your praises and petitions.

Your baby needs to hear how much you love and depend on God, because it won't be long until "anyone my Mom and Dad love" your baby will love. You won't be too surprised when he tells you in a few short years that he wants the Lord to be a personal friend in his life as he is in yours.

For now, consider God's power and love.

Study your baby's hands—his perfect, tiny fingernails, how each joint in his finger moves, his soft, delicate skin. Dream what those hands will do someday because of how you're caring for your baby now.

Worshiping God

The heavens are telling the glory of God; they are a marvelous display of his craftsmanship. Day and night they keep on telling about God. Without a sound or word, silent in the skies, their message reaches out to all the world. Psalm 19:1-3

IT'S therapeutic to revive childhood memories of standing quietly and watching a snowfall, walking in a spring rain, looking closely at the structure of a flower, sitting by a fireside and watching the multicolored flames, watching a bird taking a bath, listening to the wind pass through a pine tree. These scenes make beautiful worship experiences. They give you the chance to magnify the Lord's power, and with the stretch of the imagination, visualize yourself being there when he spoke everything into existence where once there was nothing.

When you enjoy what he created for you to enjoy, *you worship.* When you glorify the one who made the wind, rain, stars, *you worship.* When you thank him for breathing into you the breath of life, *you worship.* And when you relive the magical moment when you heard your baby take his first breath, *you worship.*

These special times with God will always be necessary, no matter what role you're living.

Do you long to have a special worship experience with God? Let you husband know how badly you need it, and make arrangements to have a brief time with God.

Your Inheritance

YOUR baby is receiving a living inheritance from you. The inheritance includes:

Acceptance: You're accepting your baby exactly the way he is, the phase he's in, the progress he's making.

Security: You're feeding him when he's hungry, changing his diapers when needed, holding him when he needs to feel your arms around him. You're sending him messages through your voice, your touch, your smile that you find pleasure in him.

Patience: You're not holding it against him personally for totally destroying any semblance of order in your life.

Integrity: You're persistent in interpreting his needs, his likes, and his dislikes.

Love: This is the lasting force when all the other gifts fail. Your love for him is unconditional.

What's your inheritance as a:
Woman?
Wife?
Mother?

Making Progress

I will bless the Lord who counsels me; he gives me wisdom in the night. He tells me what to do. I am always thinking of the Lord; and because he is so near, I never need to stumble or to fall. Heart, body, and soul are filled with joy. Psalm 16:7-9

THERE have been times when you've closed your eyes and relived, from start to finish, the day your baby was born: The trip to the hospital, using the breathing techniques you learned in LaMaze class, yelling at your husband at the height of your labor because his coaching wasn't good enough to make the pain go away. When you thought you couldn't stand the pain any longer, the doctor said, "One more push and you've got your baby."

It was quite a moment for you and your husband when both of you got to hold the baby the first time. As you felt the warmth of that new little body next to yours, you forgot the pain you had just experienced . . . almost!

Then it was time to leave the hospital. You snapped the baby in his car seat and you were off to show him his new home. He slept all the way home. So far, so good. It looked like motherhood would be a cinch.

Sometime around midnight the howls began, and you and your husband were too early into parenting to know what to do with a crying baby. You thought about calling the doctor, but when you glanced at the clock, you scratched that idea.

Somehow, you and your husband survived until sunrise. The thought you had earlier about motherhood being a cinch disappeared behind an overflowing diaper pail and a depleted supply of receiving blankets. You suspected that this was the way you'd meet each new day for longer than you cared to think.

The nights are more predictable now and you've gained lots of confidence, even when the baby cries. Motherhood still isn't a cinch, but it's better.

Reflect on all that's happened these last few weeks and months. Thank God for the way he has helped you progress in your role as a mother.

Your Job Description

Life is worth nothing

unless I use it for doing

the work assigned me by

the Lord Jesus.

Acts 20:24

MANY mothers are too hard on themselves. Possibly, it's because they don't realize they have a clear-cut job description.

Your job description includes days when you have to neglect your personal appearance, you don't get that button sewed on your husband's shirt like you promised you would, you run out of groceries because you can't find a break in the day to go to the store.

The reason you don't get everything done is because you remain faithful at carrying out the assignment God gave you the day he ushered you into motherhood. *Nothing* is more important than the assignment you're working on in your home.

This verse spells out your "assignment": "Jesus increased in wisdom and stature, and in favor with God and man" (Luke 2:52 KJV).

Jesus' areas of growth were "wisdom" (mental), "stature" (physical), "favor with God" (spiritual), "and man" (social). Logic says that these are the areas you will concentrate on as you help your baby develop into a whole person.

Read Acts 20:24 again, then check out these key words:

Nothing: "of no value."
Work: "to fashion or shape by labor."
Assign: "a service required by one's position."

Now read the verse like this: "Life doesn't mean anything unless I give it all I've got to help God fashion and shape my baby's life. This is the assignment I acquired when I reached parental status. This will continue to be my assignment until God reveals my next assignment."

Experiencing God's Love

May you be able to feel and understand, as all God's children should, how long, how wide, how deep, and how high his love really is; and to experience this love for yourselves, though it is so great that you will never see the end of it or fully know or understand it. Ephesians 3:18-19

I have loved you . . . with an everlasting love. Jeremiah 31:3

EPHESIANS 3:18-19 tells you to "experience God's love for yourself." God's love can be compared with other love relationships you've had during your lifetime.

Hopefully, you have good memories of the love your mom and dad had for you as a child. They picked you up and kissed your hurts away when you fell, carefully selected gifts for your birthdays and Christmases, helped you with homework, let you know how proud they were when you excelled, and supported you when you failed.

Your husband tells you often how much he loves you and how he appreciates what you do for him and the baby.

Friends have been generous in their expressions of love. They came through royally when you told them you were pregnant. They organized your surprise showers. They prayed for you after you called and said that you were on your way to the hospital to have your baby. They visited you in the hospital and made sure meals were brought in when you arrived home.

As important as these loves are, God's love tops them all. You'll spend a lifetime trying to express what your heart feels about that love.

Someday when your baby is old enough to talk, he'll put these words together: "I love you, Mommie." That announcement will include all the mistakes you've made and all the frustrations and impatience you've had.

Your goal of becoming the first Perfect Mother has some cracks in it, but your baby won't remember those flaws because he loves you. His saying "I love you" gives you that refresher course that keeps reminding you of God's love for you.

God loves you when you make mistakes. He loves you when you're frustrated and impatient. He knows every imperfect part about you and he keeps loving you.

Aren't you glad God knows you were born with an imperfect nature, capable of sinning, and he died for you anyway? Now that's perfect love. That's why God's love is different from all other loves, and you're experiencing that love for yourself in your Closet Times!

Changes

Except the Lord builds the house, they labor in vain who build it; except the Lord keeps the city, the watchman wakes but in vain. Lo, children are a heritage from the Lord, the fruit of the womb a reward. As arrows are in the hand of a warrior, so are the children of one's youth. Happy, blessed, and *fortunate is the man whose quiver is filled with them!*

Psalm 127:1, 3-5 AMP

EACH phase of life culminates in an event that marks the end of that phase and the beginning of another.

You stopped jabbering when you started saying legitimate words. You didn't run as much when you discovered that climbing, hopping, and skipping were more fun.

Your elementary school years lasted six years, then that phase was over. Six years later you graduated from high school. Next you decided to go on to college or pursue a vocation. Soon that phase ended.

Your single life came to an end with a twenty-minute wedding ceremony that took one year to plan. A few days later, the honeymoon was over.

Next phase. You conceived your baby and the two of you, who had become one, became three.

Enter: The parenting phase. You don't see yourself ever leaving this phase. There's a good reason for that thought. Parenting is never quite over. It has something to do with "eternity." Since it does, God wants to be actively involved during this phase. He had a definite purpose for delivering your baby. Your baby is so important that God "scheduled each day of [your baby's] life before [he] began to breathe" (Psalm 139:16). That's a heavy truth. It's so heavy that you must involve God in all the responsibilities and decisions surrounding this endless phase.

In what areas do you feel you've changed since you became a mother? Share your thoughts with your husband and ask him if he has seen other changes. He has probably changed too. Ask him how he is feeling about his new role as a father.

Imagining the Future

Train up a child in the way he should go [and in keeping with his individual gift or bent] and when he is old he will not depart from it.

Proverbs 22:6 AMP

IMAGINE what your baby will be doing when he's eighteen. What were you doing when you were eighteen?

You were in your prime. Life was good! People told you that these were the best years of your life. You accepted challenges. You made important decisions. You searched and struggled to understand God's will. The decisions got bigger and more intense as you got further into your twenties . . . a job, a life partner, and eventually a family.

How do you perceive yourself now? Is life still exciting? Still in your prime? Accepting challenges? Are you the wife you imagined you'd be? Still in love with the handsome man God designed for you?

As you work with your baby, it's impossible to know that this little one, who will soon master the sitting-up position without pillows, who will realize he was born to crawl, and who will work himself to a standing position, will, in eighteen years, face many of the same decisions you faced when you were that age.

What does it do to your confidence when you know that

what you're doing now will have a lasting influence on your baby's decisions in the future? Aren't you glad you have God to help you with your job?

Reflect on Proverbs 22:6.

Train up: dedicate.

In the way he should go: with regard for the child's character and capacity.

He will not depart: the child properly trained won't escape the influence of such training.

These *can* be the best years of your life. It's all in how you imagine them to be. Do some imagining.

What do you imagine your baby will be doing in:

Five years?

Ten years?

Twenty years?

What do you imagine you will be doing in:

Five years?

Ten years?

Twenty years?

Ask your husband to do the same imagining and compare your answers. Pray together and ask God to help you train your child the way God wants you to train him.

Developing Faithfulness

I am the Lord, the God of

all mankind; is there

anything too hard for

me? Jeremiah 32:27

The Lord will go before

you and will be with you;

he will not fail nor

forsake you.

Deuteronomy 31:8

YOU may have more in common with one of the great men of the Bible than you realize. Example: He's a shepherd in the desert of Midian taking care of his sheep. He's been a shepherd for forty years. It's a lonely job. Shepherding has become routine. He doesn't see a day when he will change jobs. His name is Moses.

One day it's different. Moses sees a burning bush that defies being consumed by fire. In the burning bush he hears God say his name. Moses starts toward the bush, but God tells him to take off his shoes because he's standing on holy ground.

God tells this ordinary shepherd that he has been chosen to go to Egypt to set God's people free. "Who? Me? I'm just a shepherd!"

But God liked Moses' credentials of faithfulness, and to get them on his resume he was given a temporary job assignment that produced steadfastness and allowed lonely times in the desert, which, in turn, gave him prime time to talk with God. He was being shaped and prepared for the Exodus Extravaganza.

God's final statement carried

Moses through some difficult times
when Moses was trying to convince
Pharaoh to let the people go. God
told Moses that he wouldn't have to
go down to Egypt and carry out this
job assignment "empty-handed"
. . . and you know the rest of the
story.

What do you have in common
with this great man of God? The day
you arrived home with your baby,
your first response to each day was
imposed on you by a hungry baby's
wake-up call. Since then, you
haven't punched a time clock and
you haven't had regular coffee
breaks. They don't come with the
job. It's routine. You don't see a day
when you'll change jobs.

Listen to the dynamics of your
job! Every day you feed, clothe, talk
to, hold your baby; you're standing
on holy ground. You are caring for a
human being who has been made in
the image of God, and your baby
has the potential of becoming one of
God's children. No one has to
remind you what's in store for
God's children.

You may not have long periods of
time to spend with God, but you
must create some times to be with
him, not necessarily long times but
prime times. Why? It's the only sure
way to overcome the sneaky
techniques of a world that works
overtime to keep you from
understanding the depth of being
faithful at your job as a mother.

During your Closet Times, you
and God plan your counterattack
against false advertising, and he

helps you ignore the distorted voices of a secular world that is opposed to family as God designed it. Those are the voices that say, "Parenting takes too much time. You've got better things to do." "Your baby is slowing you down and keeping you from being all you can be." "Your child will never express his appreciation for all you're doing." "It's not worth it!"

Closet Times help you distinguish God's voice from other voices that deter you from being the mother you know you can be. They give God time to shape you and prepare you to lead your child through each phase of his life, even when you can't see the end results of your hard work. And here's the clincher: Every time you leave your Closet Time, you know you don't have to face your God-called job empty-handed.

What two goals would you like to reach before your baby is a year old?
1.
2.

When your baby digs into his first birthday cake, come back to this page to see if your goals were reached!

For now . . . *Happy Parenting!*

scripture to memorize

When You're Fearful or Frustrated

What time I am afraid, I will trust in thee. Psalm 56:3 KJV

Fear not, for I am with you. . . . I will strengthen you.
Isaiah 41:10

Give your burdens to the Lord. He will carry them. Psalm 55:22

Live one day at a time. Matthew 6:34

Don't worry about anything; instead, pray about everything.
Philippians 4:6

Don't be upset. Expect God to act! Psalm 42:11

Don't be impatient. Wait for the Lord, and he will come and save you! Psalm 27:14

Don't be afraid, for the Lord will go before you and will be with you. Deuteronomy 31:8

When You Need Assurance

We have become gifts to God that he delights in. Ephesians 1:11

Work hard and cheerfully at all you do, just as though you were working for the Lord. Colossians 3:23

God wants his loved ones to get their proper rest. Psalm 127:2

This is the day the Lord has made. [I] will rejoice and be glad in it. Psalm 118:24

I will pray morning, noon, and night . . . and [God] will hear and answer. Psalm 55:17

Give thanks [to God] for all he is going to do. 1 Timothy 2:1

God . . . gives us all we need for our enjoyment. 1 Timothy 6:17

For when I am weak, then I am strong, the less I have, the more I depend on [God]. 2 Corinthians 12:10

For [I] know that nothing [I] do for the Lord is ever wasted. 1 Corinthians 15:58

My help cometh from the Lord, which made heaven and earth. Psalm 121:2 KJV

Teach [me] to number [my] days and recognize how few they are; help [me] to spend them as [I] should. Psalm 90:12

Because [the Lord] is so near, I never need to stumble or to fall. Psalm 16:8

Daily
Reminders

Children are a gift from God; they are his reward. Psalm 127:3

Train up a child in the way he should go [and in keeping with his individual gift or bent] and when he is old he will not depart from it. Proverbs 22:6 AMP

But when you pray, go into your most private room, and closing the door, pray to your Father Who is in secret; and your Father Who sees in secret will reward you in the open. Matthew 6:6 AMP